Munching
Mark

Mark munched and munched.

He munched on chips and candy and cakes.

3

He never munched on
carrots or apples
or bananas.

4

His dad kept saying,
"Stop munching, Mark!"

His teacher kept saying,
"Stop munching, Mark!"

Soon everyone called him
Munching Mark.

But Mark kept on munching.
Until . . .

he got a toothache.

It ached and ached.

Mom took him to the dentist.

The dentist said,
"Stop munching, Mark!"

So now Mark munches on carrots and apples and celery.

He never munches on chips or candy or cakes.

Well . . .
sometimes.